ANEMOIA

MUSINGS FROM MY NOTEPAD
FABLE

SKYLAR BLACK

ISBN 979-888555081-9

For,

the caretakers and the ones who need to be cared for.

Contents

Contents

Contents

Contents

Contents

Title

ANEMOIA

SKYLAR BLACK

Love,

SkylarBlack

Foreword

"If I read a book and it makes my whole body so cold no fire can warm me, I know that is poetry. If I feel physically as if the top of my head were taken off, I know that is poetry. These are the only ways I know it. Is there any other way?"

— Emily Dickinson, Selected Letters

Preface

The revelations and changes in a person's life can never be compared to someone else's. It is something unique and identifying, like my vulnerable poetry, or a creation hidden in drawers and coat pockets, until they fade away in the past of our universal clock. I always wonder what to put in a preface, although this is the second one I am writing. Perhaps I will keep it short this time and give you a heads up for the rocky road ahead. This book is immensely close to my heart because not only did I realize the wonders of the world in the past six months, but also discovered wonders and truths inside myself. There are people today who are unfortunately not with me today but have been a huge support throughout my life and this book is a tribute to them.

This book is also a tribute to those people who have stuck by me through these phases in my life and have forgiven and advised me whenever I lost my way. I find myself writing this on my desk in a state of more maturity than before, and I am glad to start new beginnings and a new year with something emotional, communicative and personal to me. Change and love are the two constants in the world that can take such forms that no one can ever predict or work towards. It happens and we must accept it.

I hope we can all accept something today and hope for the best!

PREFACE

- Skylar

Acknowledgements

The making of this book only came about due to the care and support I have received from the people I have surrounded myself with and have had the wonderful opportunity to know. Without them, the meaning and the outlines of this book would mean nothing but the very wasteful dust that I have arisen from.

To Mom, for being my best friend, my shopping gal and my home for 17 years. For being the best mother one could ask for. To her beautiful light and grace, to her.

To Dad, for being my life coach, my Popeye and my comfort person, all while giving me a life I know I do not deserve. For being the best role model to me. For his great wisdom and insight, to him.

To Aarav, for coming into my life as a person of joy and laughter, for giving me all his free food and charm to keep deep in my heart. For being the most annoying yet cute human being, to him.

To Moni Didi, for being there for the past 10 years, for making me laugh so loud I rolled on the floor, and for being the best sister and guardian I could ask for. To her beauty and love, to her.

To Kai, for being him, to my, her, and the they that join us. To him for being so lovely and enduring that life without him would be like

ACKNOWLEDGEMENTS

a rainbow without a violet. To his strength and compassion, to him.

To Meghana Jayaraman, for being my soul sister and favorite person in the world. To her for bringing me joy, comfort, laughter, peace and craze in a single moment and her poor cooking skills. To her burning the kitchen while boiling water and tripping over cold floors. To her wonderful eyes, to her.

To Aadit Anand, my partner in crime and food. To the memories of us walking school halls and laughing through the scrawls. To us, hiding from the world and making our own little universe. To his gift of selfless self love and wonderful smile, to him.

To Avishi Goel, my mesmerizing girl of the true dreams. To us, never knowing what to do but doing things all the same and eating weird candy and managing lives like we manage nothing else. To her, being an angel incarnate, and my close friend, to her.

To Shubham Banerjee, for being my brother from another mother but blood bound all the same. To him for seeing me through pain and sharing it with me, for making me feel worthy and being my me through everything hard. To his gorgeous mind and red scarves of love, to him.

To Momo, my handsome golden retriever, for being my constant fluffy friend and comfort. For lightening the mood when I'm down and for sharing the same obsession I have with Marie Biscuits and

ACKNOWLEDGEMENTS

Apples. To his joyous aura, to him.

To Yuti Harshavardhana , my best friend, my mentor, my childhood friend and my singing star. To her for bringing me little moments of joy and for being the brightest one out there, with her wit and artistic brilliance. To her.

To the people I have lost but gained in more ways than one, to those who have led me this way and silently hope for my greatness. As do I for them. To my close friends and family for the past 17 years, and more.

To my friends and family, to all of the people who have supported me throughout the process of my journey and have given me immeasurable love and advice that I will remember till the day I leave this beautiful world.

To my teachers for being supportive not only in my weak moments but in my great ones too. To them for making me realize the importance of knowledge and being exceptional in helping me gain and use some of it.

Lastly, to all of you, for choosing to survive and stay, for being here and making me feel like a small speck in the large commune of the world. To you for waking up another day.

To us.

Prologue

Light a candle,

 in your name.

1

Is my brain okay?

Oh wait,

That's my heart!

2

Sucked inside,

By myself.

3

Who is the maker of these thoughts?

"You", the mirror answered.

4

Darkness for the stars,

Brightness for the pain.

5

Things that I now do seem new

Why do I not know anymore?

6

Wings for flight

Join me high

Across the greens

Past the screams.

7

What does it smell like?

The scent that emits from you

Is it a yellow peach or sunflower?

Or is it a flower blue?

I guess I will never know

But I still light this orange candle

In the nostalgic name of you.

8

Beyond her smiles,

Lie all her scars.

9

You're a heartbreaker.

you're a homewrecker

You're a me wrecker

You're a cruel hecker.

Leave me alone

Love me alone

Why do I still see?

Why do I still feel this way?

Pink inked letter

Like a woodpecker

Tore through my skin

This is your sin.

I hate you

I hate your words

Nothing came true

Not even the blue birds.

I tried to cope

Tried to mope

But you still struck hard

An unspoken love card.

This feeling is messy

All my feelings hazy

But I still flash a smile

As sour as lime.

I just really hate you

I really am annoyed

But you are just so blue

Sticking to me like glue.

Just what do you want?

My heart's price not enough

My body you come to haunt

Once soft, now rough.

I've lost hope

Never had any really

But like that sliver of dope

I can't even live freely.

I hate you

Really really despise you

But you still stand here

And I still just endear.

10

I'm mad

I'm sad

I want to break you

I want to fix you.

The scream and rant kind of mad

The want to scold you kind of mad

The want to break things kind of mad

But all I am in front of you is sad.

So much frustration

So much hesitation

Only because I seem to care

Whether or not you'll be there.

My house of sand

Created by hand

How did you so easily

Take apart my very being?

You have no idea

You have no damn clue

Oh how I'm still a menace

How I'm still a fool.

Get out of my head

Get out of my bed

Just get out now

Don't want a why, what, how.

Even when I'm boiling

I look at those coiling

Waiting for your text

When you said thank you, next.

Leave my world

I can't have that

Finally say goodbye

I can't see that.

I hate this rule

Of still begin friends,

Because all I want to do

Is run away from you.

11

Words used are not necessarily words said.

Words said are not necessarily words felt.

12

Restless are those souls,

that have to be far apart.

Teary are those eyes

that can't restart.

But broken are those hearts

that will always be so far.

13

It isn't something you have to ultimately

prove.

It's just something you have to ultimately

love.

14

Why is it that it's quiet?

Why is your death so creepy quiet?

15

Reaching the breaking point

Warmer than my tears

Colder than your face

Again, I don't know what to do.

16

As she rose from the rocks

And ashes of construction

Her phoenix eyes glowed

The immortal grey sand

Around her lay bored.

17

You make me feel worthless,

You make me want to destroy you.

I hate you.

As much as the world hates me,

I hate you.

18

The world moves on

Throwing me away

My being is burnt

Under years of belief

I don't want

Any part in this

I don't want to die

But I am forced again.

19

It hits in bits

Creeping in like veins

It hits in waves

Stealing your breath away.

20

Miss me

Save me

Hate me

Kill me

Please.

21

My thoughts have destroyed me,

More than blades ever could.

22

It was not a staircase down below no more.

It was a viral body part, stuck to me like you.

23

Candles and crystals

Echoes of trapped voices

Processing as equals

Loud, scary noises

Not closeted just scared

Not black but flared

My plural self within

This therapeutic set in.

24

Come quick, silent being

And comfort broken me

That he is finally at sea.

25

Ink me like you hate it.

Break me like you know it.

Take me like you saw it.

Leave me like you want it.

26

My grey socks today

Have finally begun to match,

Your grey ashes at bay.

27

Why do I still look for you?

Everyday out of bed

All my steps into the truth

You're still floating in my stead.

My condition will worsen

This death addled prison

I still look for you now

That unfamiliar scent now.

When do you have to leave,

'Now' they all say around me

No goodbyes in store for me

No dull funeral for me to grieve.

Pieces and pieces of words and letters

I tried making them enough

But everyone is suddenly a truth-teller

There is so much more for you and I to discuss.

No waiting in the hospital

No blood red crime scene

Just words and words,

Dad, I just do not have your memories.

Even if I say I miss you

Even if I weep that I want to see you

You won't be there

You won't stand there.

I want to cross this divide,

And say a simple hello

But my crying open eyes

Don't see your angelic halo.

On a highway to that place,

My eyes finally cry,

And think as they run down my cheeks

'Will we now disappear?'

No emotional embrace for you and I

Just a promise and this vocal tune

That seems like me and myself,

I've cried like hell since noon.

With wounded limbs I run to you

Hands finally up in defeat

Not even your ashes come to me anymore

As I fall on my crying feet.

28

What is the meaning?

Of having nothing but you

As I watch your smile go,

And my paints just glow.

29

I gave you a name

I gave you a star

Then why,

Just why,

Did you scar?

30

When we are over,

When this is just me dear lover,

Will thy heart still,

With my name beat until?

31

As fresh as sea grass,

As light as jade water scent,

My hands slowly glide towards,

Your green embrace.

32

Bodices outlined grey,

Dark tiles and tapwater,

The sun sets once again,

Me reaching to you faster.

33

Symphonies are catastrophic

So why is ours so metaphorical, when

You talk in riddles and I laugh

But no one hears you barf.

You cook the same meal today

And I love you the same too,

Wondering about whether you

Deserve my lies or whether I

Deserve, slow painful death,

For my hideous, heinous crimes.

You smile at me and my heart,

Blooms as it splinters,

Breaks as I still linger.

34

I shall shed that cry

Each time my heart thinks of you,

Whether that river trough,

Will burn or let me fly,

Is a question for that time.

35

Straight down or circles?

Lightning and skies

Plastered and surround

How did you recognise,

Ater so long finally,

My forgotten face and soul?

36

Incessant ringing it was,

Advocate, so arrogant

Gleaming crippling claws,

Noisy blood so ignorant.

37

Blamed simplicity reluctant,

The blurred world redundant,

Stopped all such movement,

When erected that monument of grief,

Of blue real grief.

38

Not humans anymore

But machines,

Depths of programming

That run not on fuel

But on cold methanine.

39

Phoenix flames alight

Kindjals held tight

Owls heard behind

The seasons were never blind.

40

The trees are crying in tapestries, while

the seas pull apart each day.

But, one thing that stays in stationary

is my immobile soul, that

stopped when you cried, and the

entirety of me splintered and crashed inside.

One day, I'll find you whole and sweet, and

I'll cleave my pieces all jagged, to fix you.

My last breath will only make sesnse,

when I save you and die,

only to never finally see you shine.

41

Treachery and sins

All the claims I have made

Some false, some true

Real memories now fade.

Forgiveness I ask who

Myself or those hearts

This crazy ordeal

Not one remorse to tear apart.

A liar, a cheat

But so much a coward to fake dripped blood

And restart that flood.

She leaves with hurt

He pats my back

One who loved me be

Now cuts me no slack.

To deserve and change

Apologise to guilt

Am I to say sorry?

Or dive into victim again?

Not time to croak

All these flashy lies

Darkness, entity cloak

All I see is a human die.

To wait for thier return,

the hope I take grant

I wish thought I never see

Until I see change in me.

Two voices call

One me the other too

Should I sleep in fall,

Or learn to pull through?

42

If only I knew where I was going,

Perhaps,

This journey would be that much easier.

43

Once fate

Now nothing more than a sight that stings

Like salt in coffee,

You became bitter to me.

44

To make you happy

I become unhappy,

I knew you knew

But you still continued

And just wactehd

As the struggle became real.

45

To cry without tears

To seem tough with no fears

Get me back in lockets

For I want to now,

Swim with rocks in my pockets.

46

Two bodies, one soul

Twin flames yes, no

I killed her

Half a soul

Half a ghost

A wretch.

47

Hopeful I suppose

Grief allows us to be

But don't mistake sadness

For what joy is ultimately supposed to be.

48

It was a horrendous time,

her house with mines

that blew up with emmory

they're gone, grow up darling.

Heartbreak was physica

the bones so abysmal

it was so beautiful

only for life so simple.

heartbreak is beautiful

like frozen red tulips

those lakes burning

and her brain, humming.

she sang those songs

her tears on the ntes

her heart was strong

peace of glass they wrote.

heartbreak is loving

the only constant delight

emotions like colors forming

the rainbow in the flight.

heartbreak, an epic, an era

long nights of no cinderella

short periods of anger

overcome with adrenaline meger.

she learned it all,

the price of each emotions,

her mirror in the hall,

heartbreak s bind devotion

and she loved it, but it broke her.

49

The contents all flushed

My back against the metal

As my lips leak blood

My glass chest was forced to throw.

50

Glidng through walls and monuments,

The incandescent rage in me

Dissolved into nothing more than tears.

She was someone

I wanted to show the world

I am hoping it will be

Enough yesterday to have the place,

To wipe her blood red tears,

With my own.

51

To remember you once brought pain

Still does like uncalled rain

But, the sun only shines brighte

When I no longer want these

Fond memories

To end.

52

Kiss me once more, my love

Just so I can breathe

Since you left this October

I've forgotten my blue seas.

The sun on your skin

Brings out those golds,

In your eyes, neck and chin

As I watch you sleep.

I want to kiss you

Till the mountains crumble

And the lakes misty sing

Praises of me and you.

53

She still makes that face

the one pale and rosy

that I once fell in love with

her voice is my heart's call.

It's uncanny and red

how I am praying even today

to see her skin of snow

and kiss her under the mistletoe.

My windows are wide open

socks lad feet still cold

but her laugh is warm

and I cannot seem to move on.

To tell her my secrets

is a game I do not know how to play

How do I still want one

when my words send her away?

Until mist and dust is me

I'll love the oceans in she

and life is so bleak

but to forget her is treachery.

These grays of definition

Blocked phone calls and more

wish she would say once more

that my eyes are her imagination.

there was nothing there but strangely today,

I feel the taste of her lips

and the crevices of her soul

the cottage we made, the blanket we shared

her long black locks caressing me

just as her hands roamed free.

Intimacy in the silence,

the fire she ignited

there was nothing there

but I still hear her innocence

in the pictures I have deleted

of her flushed morning face.

My sweater on her bodice

as the breath she takes still gives me some life

so many lies and blood,

her tears have become mine.

Misery is my middle name,

cold curse in the farewell hug.

she towers over me now

even with the same height

I cower away from those hands

that once lulled me to no nightmare sleep.

pages are inked with her

in museums and palaces

her golden wings shine

as I fall for my crimes.

I can never be at peace

for she's the woman I love

eons have already passed

and our time will never come.

There was nothing there

but her curves call to me

those coffee scented sweaters

that she gives me freely.

there is nothing there still

but she holds my unclean hands

and guides me towards joy

as I give her hurt to be coy.

Nothing between us but,

our faulty tethered souls,

she is a creature of wonder,

that tastes like lemon and fruit bowls.

Her eyes hold intelligence,

more than anything else,

but the tears from them

kill me a little each time.

There is something here,

in our breaths mingling

as my lips brushed hers

and her eyes started twinkling.

54

The laughs seemed filled with tension

utter panicking tensions that is

seemingly eating away

at my fearful bones

to the blood color of my wrongs.

So much haunting and martyrdom

What have I done?

Is it me?

Or the tension in this room that thunders me?

55

You can't leave something empty and open a life chapter anew.

You can never move on without processing something that is still importanly incomplete.

56

The pencil lead did not fit

and finally the polymer cracked

like my claws and snarls

that never fit those

sweet and decadent halls.

I'll take my diadem of crones

and pray to the maiden

but it is the mother,

who grant my wishes to molten.

57

Tie me up in chains,

chains of rusted iron and lead,

shackle my bodice in ropes

ropes of tropical thorn and jute

drape me in blood,

blood of my own skull and bones

till even my spirit can't get away.

Drag those talons deeper

under the sea of flames

erupted but suffused.

Kill me like a traitor

and let the bruise

maim me so red

that even the lady of death

starts to cry.

58

Ages later, when my soul

Is all but ink, my love

Will still exist for you.

59

If it's not something you got on your own,

then you

will never entirely

have what was never

rightfully yours,

even people.

60

Spread apart for them to see

like the sacred Virgin Mary

but it's not angel blood red,

just demonic black ichor

set those nails on my skin

and paint me pale gray.

I like the the numb ache

because I deserve it this way

my wrath will eat you up

after the jutted bones and battle scars

become my bare jewelry

and I'll stalk your death call.

Suffrage and screaming

you'll pay for with pleas

that will never reach

my universally bound ears.

61

it seems muddy but clean

the roads I have never been through

maybe my soddy footprints

will make it something discovered

perhaps,

something new.

62

She's so divine and bright

caressing my falling tears

it's so nice here mom

I can see you fly, you fly.

Can you guess again today,

all the secrets in me

how did you always know

but now you cry, you cry?

Please by my mother today

give birth to me again

I want rejoice for you

And so much more time, more time.

You will leave won't you,

in two room without hugs

I can't reach for you again

so now we both cry, both cry.

63

He ignores my love,

she thinks it something else

but I still remember it,

the horrid and putrid smell

of that cage of misery

that I still stay in,

for all my eternity.

64

ruptures become cracks

cracks become shifts

shifts become cataclysmic

but then why is our love,

still so toxic?

and not beautiful or cosmic?

even after I broke you apart

and you cracked my raptured heart?

65

The colossal buildings will die

the glacial rivers will burn

the vapid rocks will ash

but I will never break.

I am the rock against

which the aqua breaks,

I am the soil against

which the earth is remade.

I will never break.

I am immortal.

In soul, in the wholes

of the universe so big.

I am the universe,

in atoms that you will never find.

66

Jagged and barren hills

make homes for the today

and yet your porcelain face

can never make a happy day.

Behind those forest eyes

lie the secretes that you hide

that attack the heart

like arrows of poison,

but so invisble apart.

67

Who do I ask for validity?

Who is the right reliability?

Can you determine my worth

Like you do at her birth?

She may never learn

The lessons of the sun

For your critical knife,

Will never let them thrive

Who fade away like pearls,

In the hopes of keeping humanity alive.

From you,

For you.

68

It is the choice that makes us,

and it is the choice that will be unmade.

69

My thoughts are like paint. If only I knew how to paint them into
a story.

70

We fell because it was breathtaking.

We crashed because we refused the truth.

I was broken because you picked yourself up and,

I realised, I had been so blind.

71

All hearts are not pumping

All souls are not pretty

All songs are not romance

All money is not class

All love is not real.

72

Me, myself and I. I am not an introvert. I feel an abyss of storms, but you do not see it. You never will. Because unlike angelic ones, you will never realise, how stuck up you are, in your own sluggish life.

73

They were right there. Whispering, conversing.

I was there too so why is it so blurry now?

This phone flashlight is shining really bright on me.

My head throbs, my bones ache but it is still so blurry.

I felt myself spiral.

I still am.

But, why am I still so quiet about it?

I want to talk about me.

I want to be narcissistic.

I am a narcissist.

I am a hypocrite.

I am a disaster.

I am an attention seeker.

I am every bad thing the world says I deserve.

And I could not agree more.

74

Strangely for those pleas

Never before light at the end

The dusty road had been no stop,

But today, I reached out again.

75

Shoes untucked and socks wet,

I walked through the music with rain

Earphones falling with each step,

The sky was bright soon again.

76

The world was spinning,

The ropes holding me in place

Giddy giggles escaped

I was hopeful once again.

77

Why is it so easy for me to go back there? Back to that place of no life, where only pain festers, where I seem to always suffer? Why is it so easy to go back there, even when it doesn't help at all? Even when nothing good ever comes out of it. It is because that is the easy way out. Even if it were easy, why is it so hard to accomplish? Why is it so hard to even comprehend? This is not me anymore. I am not me anymore. What have I done? What have I done? This is all just too much. so much. too less. I did so much, achieved so much, and yet, I am so messed up. I'm still so lost. so scared. Of both tomorrow and that no lit place, where all the broken hearts go. Am I good enough? Enough to do something today? Was I ever enough?

78

Just a little more, one slice, one push. Just a little bit and it's over. This menace of life will end. If I am to go, then why do I sit and write this? Why am I still holding on? My heart cracks in three to leave. Do I want to leave? Must I leave? This off switch is trembling. I just don't know what it is that my shattered one is. I hate my hope, the same hope my head gives me, without any showcase of action.

This is all too much for me.

79

I am running out of time. I am really losing my mind. Everything hurts, my eyes no longer able to put up that steel wall. These feelings have finally, finally become the reason to ruin me.

Please stop. The voices scream and are so loud, booming through the memories alighting in vapid flames of coal. I deserve so much but death, so less but hope and you, to see you once again. Are you up there waiting, up in the skies for me? Because my shuddering arms move now and I know nothing can stop my undoing.

80

In this crazy, stupid world, among the hurdles and the sweaty hard work, lies a secret place of happiness. And by making me happy, by making her eyes bright and kind, smile europit, the place grows; we grow in mood, and the golden rays of moonshine mingle with the sun. It's more than making our own stories count; it's making them count, all f us count and love, love and love. Something ends, something for each day we wake up with a rose beside us, with the wafting scents of lemony glades and carved woddy cones.

Love, just as you deserve it.

Live, just as you pictured.

81

Why was it so overwhelming? Why is it still so overwhelming? It's not just fear that eats my flesh and stone. But lazy, paralyzed confusion that lu.ls the racked and tattered body of mine.How do we mean this? To tell the world that I am different. To tell and think and think, 'Is it even real? Am even real?'

I'm tired of the ploy and the web I play, for myself, with myself endlessly. This is angering, this is saddening, this is maddening. rever my roles. Reverse my soul, and I'll be gone.

Pleasant mind, gone forever.

82

Felt myself spiraling again. Saw it framing in my head. Cracked paint and dewy humid scents on my walls, around my own tall. I saw it all. somewhere far, forget all those memories. Desperate measures, but to no avail; the thought pushes me away instead. Slow hands moving across this page. the same tunes on repeat. same words, some letters, again and again and again. Tired eyes drop to my tears, my nose losing it's ability to give me life; my tongue bland, and tasteless.

The urge to change, splatter color across walls and my hair, to become someone else entirely, but my ears are so loud, my legs smooth, frozen solid, no steps I can take now.

I wanna be able to. So why don't they move on? Why do I just not do it? Not confused, just blank. Like someone swiped the will right out of me.

I did, I took it all.

And burnt it alongside the waters of that dark, soul-less river. For you.

83

We felt lonesome

On that steep ladder of guilt

but with his eyes of pride

the pillars became easier to reach.

someday maybe,

I'll come back for the view

to visit what seems new

but today all I take back

is a picture of the birds

that make me sing my love

for everything I do deserve,

Life did flash before me

with each rusted step I took

But the air above was cool

As warm as the dignified sun.

This is all I think of

of the freedom in this air

that hugs me like his scent.

as we make our way to earth

and even hear the trees

sing those songs of fresh leaves,

That makes me want to forever stay.

84

I realize my privilege

Traveling in a car with leisure

But my flanor searches for the sweat

That the greens of this village emit.

The family I love is laughing

And I know they would agree

That these hawkers sitting outside

Deserve more than this rocky muddy side.

The palm trees hover over green water

And my soul hovers over those blankets

That lady sells on the road side

And I want nothing more than to give her one for herself.

Raw primitive life,

Raw primitive love,

Is so much simpler than our world

And this car ride is the way,

I will ever witness this beauty,

Of this peaceful mini city.

I wonder if they struggle

As much as we don't

But they seem content and happy

As much as the privileged, the opposite.

My ankles would surely sprain

If I walked their rocky paths

But with the music of their soothing life

Even my warm bed can't match it.

Just one small community

Bound by place

But protected by hearts

That beat as one, for one.

I want this life,

Without the knowledge of the world,

So that for a split second

I feel large enough,

To surpass the enormity,

Of our looming doom.

I think I'm teary now,

For understanding so late,

That simplicity lies in the ground

And not in those heavy wings

I once dreamed to have.

This is the happiness I seek

The one so profound

That even those saints and angels

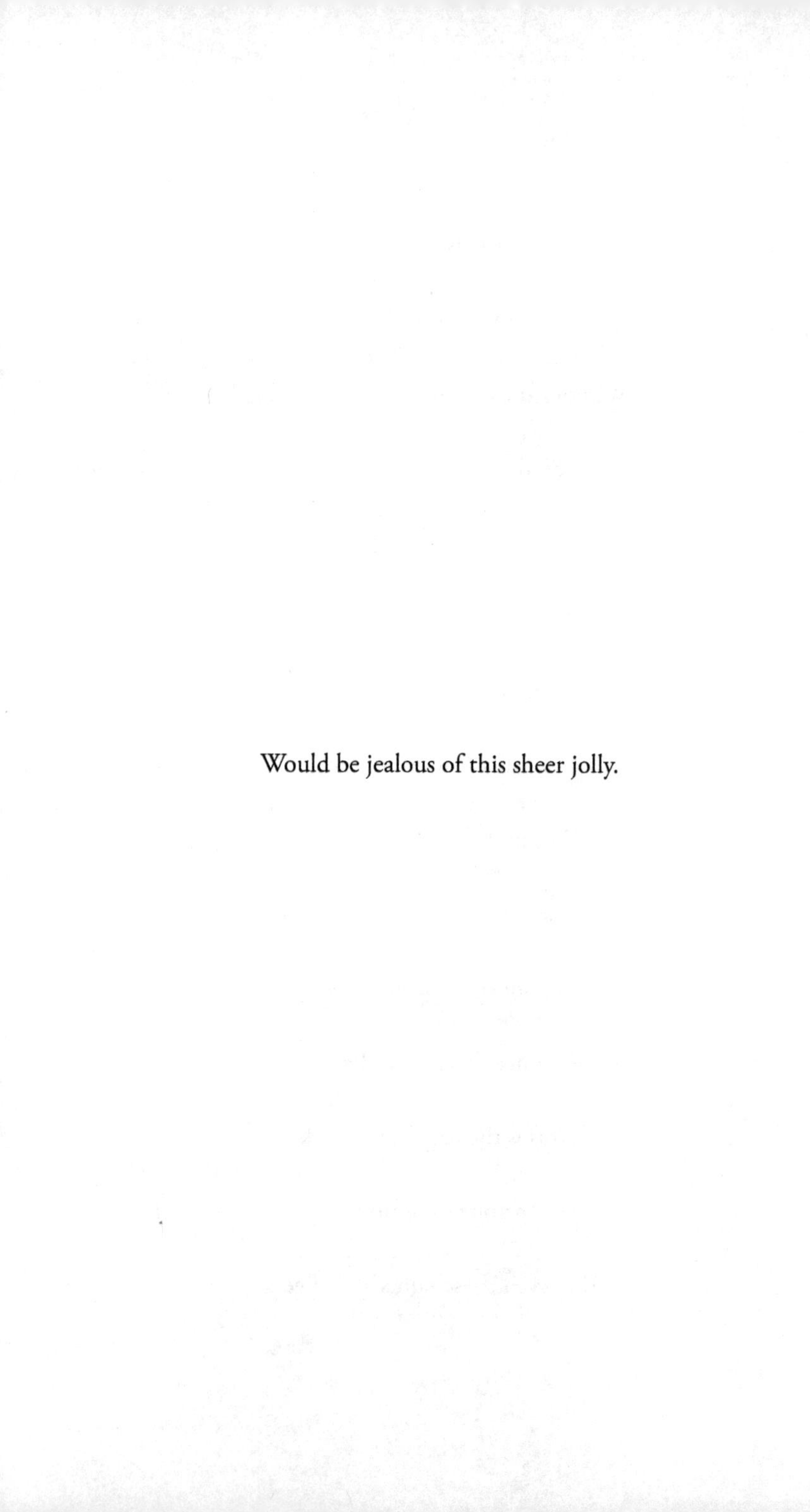

Would be jealous of this sheer jolly.

85

There are moments when I wonder

If anything we ever do

As humans and robots

Will ever be

Enough to satisfy those

Who never satisfied,

Like we are supposed to.

Their hearts never melt

From the heat of our tears

It's not a facade of our guilt,

But who's to tell them,

That the things we do

And the laughs we force through

Are ones they can never achieve.

Same old story of practice

Same old blockage of what makes me smile

But yet again I try and try

To show them and not be

A simpleton in this mockery

But a vigilante of perfection,

For their gossip and parties.

I don't blame them at all

But still the pain soars high

Everytime I see the ignorance

In their hearts and their stones.

86

Deny the thrum if you dare

destroy all your evidence of folly

devastate years of happiness

deny that you ever met my smile.

Horrible things have happened today,

horrendous words have broken out

how lovely I realize your smile is

honestly directed at someone else.

My virtues deny me the right

my principles knew what was spite

mundane attention you manipulated

mother above, just want you to shatter.

Curse my soul black and blue

close the sheath of the knife,

come closer to maim and bruise darling

curious I am to see how you make me hate you

I'm laughing in ragious temptation

of your disastrous picture of my imaginary

Where was the bitter truth for me and you?

Print a note of bedecked wealth for me

Is how low my knees have sunk,

Cruelty knows no bounds in my vigor

But I pledge to hurt you, one day demolish you,

And me too.

87

What she did would forever be here sin,

What she now admitted would be her final call for peace.

88

I see you there, but you do not smile. And slowly I see that none of us do. Forced to with issues, no tissues, only derogatory misuse.

89

Decadence is disaster, vain is our master.

90

Dining halls and mirror walls, yet not one jewel here sparkles like you do.

91

The sky is my home but now,

you hold my heart into your own.

92

If the bell tolls at skyfall again,

I hear I will believe the conjecture

That heavens you are worth to me

And I you dahlia scented one.

93

It is apathy

That my numb gives

Long gone the smiles

Long gone the time

Right when you left.

94

Abstract brush strokes

The lilies on canvas flows

But the nightingale with lamps

Are when you look the best.

I would succumb my all

For a speck of your time

To adjoin our bodies together,

So my eyes can gasp for you

As yours twinkle forever.

95

Cracks in my porcelains

The fissure of burning glass

Roses and Acacias I see

And the smell of ash I breathe.

The flames twist into me

Like vines of gossamer

A legend on portraits

Face covered by acorns

But those lace on fingers

Reflecting the love I never had.

Such gross decadence

Simply for the mess of my heart

But my sunrise today began,

With your lovely name.

96

The tapestries fall around us

Silhouettes show me with you

But my clambering heart refuses to believe

That your golden body is flushed against me.

Like the setting crimson sun,

Your sheer comes undone in my hands

And the velvety touch of my skin

Burns past us, colder than my chilled fingers.

It's a draft of a sort

Unhurried and unfinished with errors

But the taste of your laughter is in my breath

And your heart beat is steady inside.

It's almost rhythmic and twisted

The mix of so many feelings,

But when the tunnel vision clears

Your eyes are what I remember the most.

The curves of your corset untangle

And my eyes flutter as your hair sways

The perfect cosmic creation now at the peak

And your lips are on mine as it ends.

It does not end apparent

For our entangled souls under mattresses

Feel more intimate than your rosy blush

As I let slumber finish us once more.

97

Some Days it's like a bright star,

His invisible smile on me.

Most days it's just dark under my table,

The wolves circling me.

The empty mattress,

Rid of all its sheets,

I sit and feel,

Feel all those emotions buried within,

Cold in the summer,

Rainy now that it's a bummer.

Now windows just empty space

The stars are what I want

But the beeping light of my alarm

Wakes me up alas.

Torn denims, people flying

As the birds sit and eat

No one with pedigree.

Blurred vision, I see

Hands moving, I see

So much,

So much,

Blurred vision I see.

98

It's time to awaken my soul

The dark seeping thing inside

Blood red lips and kohl eyes

My wealth you use for crime.

I cackle in your rumbling

The storm exceeding your cage

I beckon the storm that will burn

The mask you have will break.

Traditions of good always wins

It bores the story now dear

How tame you all heroes are

Yet I still stand for you to fear.

99

My eyes follow the air I breathe

Transcendent shadows the winter emits

Landing upon jaded lilies in greens,

They sway like a rhapsody in a symphony.

Ancient jagged glass panes shine

The gold of the entire sun

As those white petals bloom to full again

To worship that chime, I sigh.

Will my legacy be denied?

Or will it be so dim and grotesque,

That the halls of this english library

Will enclose my words in a meticulous hurry?

Reflective falls holds me stranded and blind

As the ballads of a deeply rooted ache thrive

And me legs step closer to the lapping waters

On which those floating beauties lay.

We say breathtaking as magic

But neither the lilies nor I today

Fail to release exhales intertwined,

The water caressing my lonely, lost feet.

It's a chilly december evening,

My messy hair dry and floaty,

Wish I could give my promiscuous love

To the lilies that now surround my heart's vision.

Celestial, these flowers and lives

How physical their touch ignites into my organs,

And the here after gets decided for me

To see those lilies but oh disdain, to never be able to feel.

100

A day will end tomorrow

And with my fears I will blink away,

All my curios love for you

So as to never find this joy again.

The ridiculous sarcasm I wish this was, washes away like a
tumultuous tsunami.

But my panting heart looks on from the cliff

With nothing but rage boiling your kiss away.

The wine I am drowning in

Reminds me of the shape of your velvet gown

You wore when we danced and laughed

Before you threw away the key after locking me.

I want your genius and impeccable thoughts

To lull me to smile once more,

You wicked grinned one how lovely

Are you happy leaving me broken and lonely?

A pariah of romance I have become

Only to feel your pristine magenta gloves

Curl into my wrinkled fingers in mock care

But foolish mind of mine yearns for you still.

A whisper of my love this is

All that I have left for you

But worry not your freedom will fall tomorrow,

When you are not even a painful memory.

101

The valleys of my heart now stitched and sewn

Declare an innocent testimony of insolence

As the judge and jury point their stare at me

And I have nothing but the bloody truth to give

Yet I will never find someone like you,

But I plead guilty in the name of your murder.

You hung yourself high up in the celestial clouds

And the look of your lifeless brown orbs still haunt

And how do I explain the drought in my own

When not even a reason or declaration

You left in my heartbroken stead.

Why loved one, why did you leave me here stranded?

They sink you into the ground whilst I simply drown,

And I clutch your memoir tight in my palms

Finding it only disturbed memory and torn paper like,

So no one looks towards my soaked clothes as you go

But how do I live with knowing, sunshine

That my venom numbed your curated bones?

The greystone walls emit a fragrant cement air

And the window brings in the salt from the sea,

Wafting into my senses like your show face,

Caressing my hands to relentless dreamy slumber,

Where our room does not reek of caked blood

And the sun makes our bodies glow, together forever.

This is my destruction and catastrophe,

My last cry for your delicate call on my chapped lips,

As the days pass by in solitary darkness,

And I beg to the lonely perpetrators above,

To take me to your angelic wings if peace

So I can fall to my knees and be with you,

Just once again.

102

Never in my short minuscule days

Have I seen such shades of blue and tangerine musk

As the clouds call out their tears for the leaking night

And the sun, in all of its unfamiliar bright glow, bids me a lovely
goodbye.

My feet remain stuck in moss and frothy bubbles

As crabs shine their smiles on me and I lay sitting here,

Wondering if the crashing tidal god below,

Loves and cries for his sun lover of gold too.

It has a different scent of salt here

On that I know I will always miss

Because the rocks that give me support and lift my legs today,

Are forever gone when my tears take me home.

The sun now looks deeply red, perhaps shade of pinkish crimson,

But all I see in its frame of no corners,

Are the gloomy clouds that turn navy above,

And glisten with such beauty that we can't help but rage and cry.

It's going, oh please why does it?

As my hands shake and my heart thunders with the crashing
waves,

It's half into that horizon so lovely

That even the earth itself does not stop its rotation.

The cold water laps at my feet in panic

Of the lost brilliance for another hour of day

And it ends by groaning and thrashing against the greens,

That helped me share this abysmal heart ache.

I'm not alone I realize,

And I will never be again,

When we all come here to miss and reminisce

This beautiful flaw of nature again.

The incandescent glow of the moss and ferns,

Wash away like a wilted bark,

That floats about as I scrawl on yellow sand

But do not leave me behind my brand.

It's one in the millions of stars now,

Lost in that oceanic space that I can never visit

But the call of that boat and the sound of my heart

Will never be able to leave that picture amiss.

I want to step into the sandy seas,

And walk and drown till I reach the depth

For I know my melancholic heart,

Deserves only the depths of the cold start.

It's gone, friend and lover of mine,

Gone like seasons and colors and people

And I fear for the soul I breathe through for thrill

That I will lose a part of me, till time I see it until.

It's loud and silent in a moment of parallels,

The lights coming up again after their break

But I wait from this moment on for you,

And until the gift of the universe comes back again.

The sand tickles my limbs in my seat

And I feel my spine collapse and restructure

Just as the laws of this magnanimous civilization

Trap me in before I hug the skies once more.

The wind in my ears whoosh in the hums of a slumber

A slumber so deep and meditative

That I'm bound to realize into my abyss and chaos

That this world is too large to be wholly mine.

As are you wise eyed, elegant one,

And as am I , the dust that covers your toes and ankles

Just as the fresh minerals did today

For me and you, in my broken heart, mending with the sun, for you.

103

It's like a cataclysmic mix of kings and commoners,

Like a jaded emerald realizing it's worth with diamonds

The granite walls cut so sharp and great

How did they make me so faint?

I know now the beauty of those halls so old

The lakes that lay covered with blossoms and petals of lotuses,

Will make my eyes shine and tears fall,

For the doors that reach skyfall.

The music through the pillars,

The wooden creations so intelligent

Within it lies the act of humanity and love

That still seeps through these stones.

Deep in this small town it is,

This temple created for faith

My heart is in disbelief for the truth still

But the lives of the people come and gone,

call to me from deep within.

I'm taking something back in my bag

Sweets and wood and glaring warmth

And the shining creatures that cover the land

Of this huge sandalwood temple so grand.

A culmination of ages and conquests,

My mind mingles with the lamps that must have brightened the way

For the flames of this shrine for those kings

That paved their willful prayer.

Gold and jewelry and so much vermilion

The sheer wealth of this old dead place

Will stay alive long after we go

For the ones who made it will never die.

Tears of grief for those dead and betrayed

But a smile of peace for their souls,

As I make a promise to the carved flowers here

To return and return and return,

Till these temples are dust and I am air once more.

Epilogue

I witness the first sunrise of this year

Witness the merges of cobalt and vermillion

And the roads fade away to miles

My heart is still hammering away with the syllables of you.

The fear of forgetting how you sound,

I cut out everything that makes me sane,

I've regretted my love for you,

I will force love the pain my love gives when I think of you.

I'm closing my exhausted eyes,

The memories of your laugh resonating in my gut

As I choke down the sob in my throat

And dream of visiting the mountain top with you.

I know the love you have for words

The way you smell of Roses and vanilla

That scent does not reach my nose anymore

Neither do your warm hands caress mine.

Hours into a new beginning yet,

I'm carrying your pictures in my cortex still

You have become one with me dark haired one,

For you are the nucleus to my atoms

And I can't possibly function without you now.

The sun slowly rises from it's sleep behind the clouds

And I recall your love for these bright sunny days

Where the world seemed to stay happier for a while

And your words brought me back to wanting this life.

I realize after much distance from you,

That the life I wished with you,

Is one of unreal dreams and ambitions

One that I now know I will always want, but never have.

You are somewhere in my breath,

Somewhere stuck between peace and hell

And the road that leads to my death,

Is the end of your misery from me.

It's brilliantly yellow, this goddess friend of mine

And you look elegant in yellow too, my queen

As bright as the sunflowers I've wilted

And as grand as something way past my reach.

Is this a love story or a broken friendship?

Perhaps both for I was the one who left you,

Betrayed you and left you hanging,

For I am the one who irrevocably fell in love with you.

A pond passes by me,

Shimmery and reflective for the landscape around it,

The cesspool of mirrors and decadence,

Like you, my hamster eyed one.

Smitten is a negative here when,

I was simply one of the many losers,

Who realize your incredible worth

And know not to manage it with care.

I have let you go from my dark

To live the life of simplicity and travel

For I love you and have loved you so,

Too greedy but unworthy, so I let you go.

I shall sleep now

Under this hard leather that is not soft as your skin

And dream of rolling green hills and huge skies of love,

Where you and I darling,

Are no longer far away but making each other feel alive.

A place where my wishes if your touch in mine,

Is not a thought for another time,

But one call away

As you respond with that shy red flushed smile.

For I love you so, and have loved you from the existence of us,

For I will love you until the day they decide

That we were broken from each other

And were nothing but two lost souls ruining one another.

Oh brown eyed one, for I love you,

Have loved you since I saw your twinkling gleam,

And I will love you forever too.

Self Notes

#Self- reflection is fulfilling.

Jot down something you like. Or anything at all.

Thank You

A huge thank you to my support system, my readers, and to the ones who give kindness everyday.

I tend to write too much here, but I'm keeping it short this time.

Hope this book was as scintillating to read as it was to write it.

To a great year ahead and hopeful resolutions and changes.

From one mending, hopeful heart to the other,

Love,

Skylar

私の家族

A family I never knew I needed but am glad to have found.

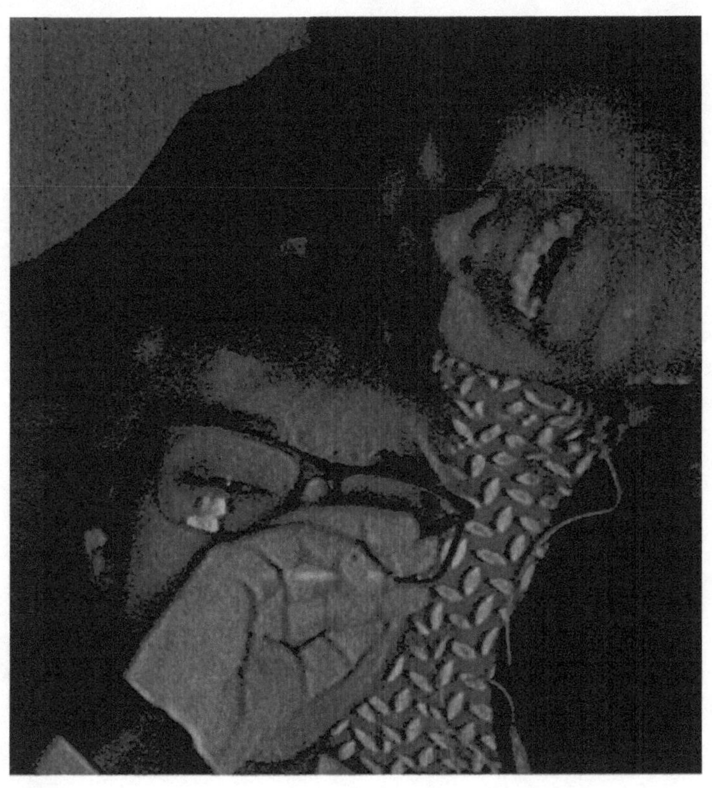

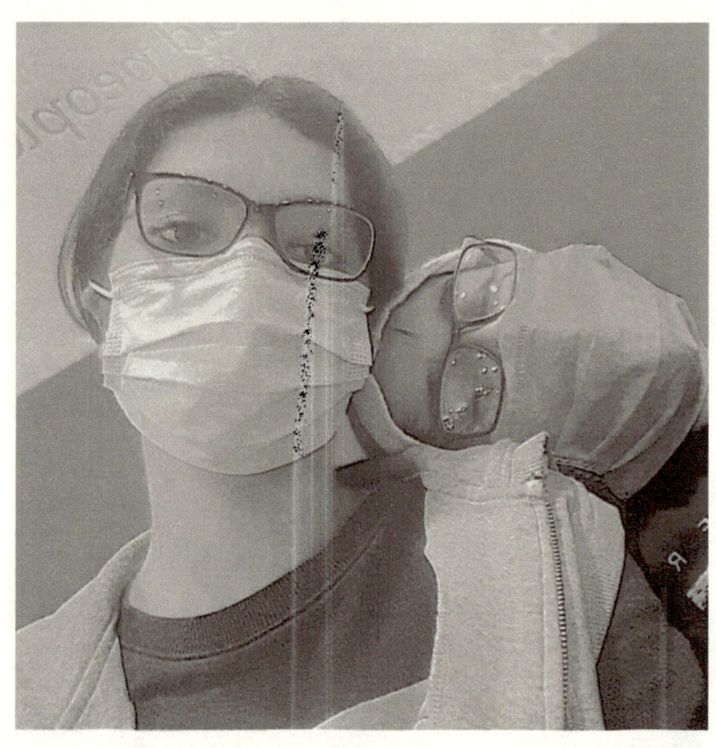

About The Author

Skylar is an aspiring 17 year old writer with a head full of dreams. Self-taught and published, she chronicles her life using simple poetry and layered verses to describe her life as a teen in a new modern world with its fair share of depth and emotions.

She is also an avid bookworm with much love for animals, especially her pet retriever, Momo.

With much experience in art forms and creativity such as painting, singing, dancing and occasionally lazing around, Skylar looks at the world like art, an interpretation of beauty.